THE SAINT OF BURNING DOWN

THE SAINT OF BURNING DOWN

POEMS BY NICOLE CUDDEBACK

Zoo Press

Zoo Press • P.O. Box 22990 • Lincoln, Nebraska 68542
Printed in the United States of America

Distributed to the trade by The University of Nebraska Press
Lincoln, Nebraska 68588 • www.nebraskapress.unl.edu

Cover: *The Temptation of St Anthony* c. 1500 by Hieronymus Bosch,
central panel, Oil on wood, Museu Nacional de Arte Antiga, Lisbon

Cover design by Janice Clark of Good Studio © 2003
www.goodstudio.com

Cuddeback, Nicole, 1967-
  The saint of burning down : poems / by Nicole Cuddeback.-- 1st
ed.
     p. cm.
  ISBN 1-932023-01-1 (pbk.)
  I. Title.
  PS3603.U34S25 2003
  811'.6--dc21

                                        2003012718

zoo017

First Edition

Acknowledgments

Grateful acknowledgment is made to the editors of the journals in which some of these poems, or versions of them, originally appeared:

32 Poems: "One Evening"; *Antioch Review*: "On the Library Window"; *Cimarron Review*: "Losing My Italian"; *Cream City Review*: "To My Left Hand"; *Ekphrasis*: "Crown for *Piazza della Santissima Annunziata*"; *Global City Review*: "Photograph and Clock at 8 p.m."; *Gulf Coast*: "Double Sonnet, Failed" and "Tyrrhenian"; *Laurel Review*: "Corleto"; *Paris Review*: "Son of Medea," "Some Lines to the Waves," and "Geppetto"; *Ploughshares*: "The Nun on the Bus"; *Poet Lore*: "Grapefruit"; *Prairie Schooner*: "Florida" and "The Rite"; *Quarterly West*: "The New Husband"; *River Styx*: "Robert Capa's Last Photograph"; *Seattle Review*: "Safe" ("The Cobbler"); *Sonora Review*: "The Divorce"; *South Coast Poetry Journal*: "Last Trip to Florida"; *Southern Poetry Review*: "Memory on a Sleepless Night" ("Pavement, Italian"); *Western Humanities Review*: "Celadon Water Dropper, 11th Century Korea" and "Arachne."

I also wish to thank Nell Altizer, Antonio Ambrosio, Susan Davis, Andrew Feld, Valerie Haskell, Edward Hirsch, Richard Howard, Judy Laberteaux, Leslie Richardson, Tracy Stroder, Pimone Triplett, Erin Van Rheenen, James Wheatley, Adam Zagajewski, and my family for their guidance, encouragement and generosity during the work on this book.

In memory of my grandparents

Table of Contents

III

I

The Nun on the Bus, Florence

Black drape like a solid shadow,
as if the shade won't slide from her. Veil,

abstracted hair lifting on the breeze.
Around us heels, furs, and scarves like swatches

of a Las Vegas, twitch of liner
on a pair of eyes, men in the cut of coats,

the usual, long-faced inspection
of each other's clothes; mine unpressed, I creep

toward her. I like her sandals, try
to look at what she sees: flitting gardens,

cracked salmon, fitful ochre, moon-green
olive leaves, the massings of over-cast days

in the age-blown stone. I follow her
off the bus and, in black wind-blasts of her gown,

move a finger out where it might be
skimmed by that day-lit, midnight tempest

descending to the piazza.
As she hurries toward San Marco and folds

into the heavy doors, I don't move.
The boy beside me watches a beauty

going by. Suspended and free
of intent, he pauses before resuming his stride

negotiating the crowds that course
between the pleasant and the tragic.

A snatch of blue above a broken wall.
The being picked up and swiftly returned.

Celadon Water Dropper, 11ᵗʰ Century Korea

Evening on the beach: no guessing
fume flood shore, all blotted the same;
nowhere leads to certainty.

Faithful copy of the daubed ends of days
before the moon shatters the swells
to a million eyes blinking in the dark.

*

You never know how it will come out.
The flow-blue may blacken, the belly
crack, mouth smash in the ashes. I sit

in flickers, my hands' heat leaving me
for the clay so that they're cold as earth,
not warm as what's inside my robe.

I balance pots on stones, close them in
with fire, I who have lost so much,
so many. I sell them cool, empty.

*

The glaze avoids, vexes surfaces
—but has a net just caught a harbor
that nearly ebbs? Infuriating, fragile

pot of blur, just for dampening ink.
Over it all, under, perhaps, ripping
cloud and sand kicked-up in the shallows.

*

We need more words for sky,
more clouds of rabbit-fish or rhino-hen
to drown the pounding nothingness.

Is death like this, or is it life?
Ancient milky-green reticulum,
mouth open for water, formed

from earth, fired to a lasting cry,
then the guardian veil of shapeless air
surrounding it all: waiting, poised.

Burying the Treasure

Search from the dining car: a tunnel,
Vernio, power lines, something yellow
blooming, gum wad on the window, black-blooded
green of cypress. Swallow the pear seeds;

focus where the hills are bare, but traffic
islands also do the trick. Disembark
at both extreme and common; the air
should have some wind in it, however,

as over thirsty hillsides of Greek islands
where the grapes grow in tufts against the sand.
Pour wine to the mark at just before
the day enters the dream of it. Then dig

with nails, pencils. Scoop with shoes. You must
get dirty if you're ever to come clean.
As if you plant yourself, feel the death
already in you. Risk you won't take root.

Wring out your head; let it pelt the bottom
of the ditch. Now every word pronounced
will be the map; each bath, distraction. No
afternoon enough. But divorce yourself

from finding. Safe, it might thicken to Atlantis,
far dearer than it was, stewed in isn't.
Toss down all you've won, stolen. Loose your gods.
Then flutter down the pictures of your dead.

Fill with earth, its wisps of faded plastic.
The life you have waited for is starting.
Study tourists, immigrants. Expect nothing.
Grow intimate with failing. Hoe your patience.

Know that you've done something good. Cut open
a brown bag, light a candle. Old-fashion, draw,
like an island of broken paths, your blue-veined heart.
Drive the coasts and highlands at that flame.

The New Husband

At sundown bats flurry round the rooftops
like flustered angels. Blessing isn't easy.

As a child in the soup of the Gulf,
how the mouths of fish bumped along my shin.

The lingering of those slick forms at the skin's verge
seemed like a grace, a border world tapping

for that thing alone in the body. Tonight I see
it's solitude I've forgotten. Without it

the loneliness brims. The shipwreck sun dips
as the doors of the drab balconies open

like night blooms, and the bats sort their black-outs
of divine and diverge. Whatever it is they do

they let it look like recklessness.
Lashing the dusk to the fish-boned crosses

of antennas trolling the heavens, the bats veer
around the wire as if reeling in

on pieces of cages. Jagged wounds retraced
all night, nearly touched, nearly crashed through to.

Tonight I'm raw as the twilight, craving
crash. Wholeness. Blunder of some featherless wing.

On the Library Window

Coy, novel vandalism, ghost
of a snapdragon blooming on the border

between the inner and the outer,
nearly lost in the separation:

a kiss on the library.
Or the library's lips upon the lawn,

down the red slide of the canyon.
Moth of a kiss still there despite how

kisses never stay. Mouth where
breath risks word, and pane

where, eyes outside, you're shut in—
but now the lips merge with lit leaf

and shadow, shuffling: gust of wish
caught in books of branches, comma—

cloud—confused. Just as dreams hover
without the weight of wit, a breach

of clarity floats between the flesh-prints
as they circle, defy the nothing,

thrilled, delinquent, longing—
Kiss me. Let me out. Stay.

Caravaggio Paints *Narcissus*

The naked knee's the first thing you see,

balled on the bank to a white-hot coal.
Or to an unformed head, sockets: moon-seas.

I tumble heady daffodils of sleeve

from his shoulder to his satin-banded elbow
that pours a perfect forearm into the hand

already lost in the original folly

of thirst, of cold reflections. Narcissus
is crouching to drink, and a vast omega

slams into and fuses with itself, there,

in the water, *the end* that it insists on
dissolving in the endlessness of circle:

half tugged to the muck of gravity; half

suspended in the chiaroscuros past
omega. His left hand, scooping, dips into

the one below, crude fist opening, glinting,

into a cupola of hand while his right palm
and fingers press at their reflections as in prayer.

The void Narcissus gathers in his arms

echoes the hungry hole inside those hands
that almost pray. Slipping through the pupil

of the mud, he's discovering there is

no *complete*, an alabaster brow of flash,
and the rest plunges back to darkness deeper

than reflection. This is the first time he's seen

himself, the stifling skin that's held him in,
and understands it's all there is to life

—then breezes rib it over, silk of thought

running, ruining. How can he look up
to the blindfold sky now? God could never be

as clear as this dark shimmer on the border

where those unswimming fingers test the air . . .
I'd thought he was the devil dressed like me!

But then I saw that I was simply he,

leaning with such terrible weight against
my lonely knee, numb like the heart pressed, pressed

to fist, to blaring knuckle, poison bulb

of asphodel, lent lily, alternating
with the weightlessness of water-weeds below

or above. Scent of sweat and freckled snails,

spirit waking. The unbearable love
in the paralyzed jonquils, early spring.

The wet color combusts, the burning turning

into his parched mouth. The candles of my bones
consume me. *Both arsonist and scorched,*

forever thirsty. That's me there, painting.

To My Left Hand

Daughter not sent to college.
Watch-laurelled, fingernails smooth and whole.
   Clean, weak, not callused. Equal
on keyboards but not in creation's
   noble scrawl.

   You live the life of a cat
asleep in rush-hour sun. Your fingers
   wander regions of the thigh;
blue shoots of ink bloom on the right hand:
   you scrub her.

   You mind Right's cuts, look on as
she jots down absurdities, constructs
   mad misspellings. Zones tingle
which she cannot reach. You tap unheard.
   Lost, she hangs

   desperate above the page.
If you write, you ache. But as one might
   rap at the base of a jar
that seems empty, you tap till she hears
   and descends.

Photograph and Clock at 8 p.m.

It's months since I've caught myself between the alarm clock
and photo of that town tilting on cliffs that drop to the gray

       border on the blue where objects are filed and filed. Again
       I've caught my fingers adding wayward hours to the night,

past the ocean, Spain, while that buckling shore keeps far off . . .
Two a.m. there now: muttering waves, lit brows of piazzas,

       slope where I slept with nightmares, tired when the pink
         mornings
       crumbled over stucco and chrome coffee bars stacked in tiers

that watched the sea. Stones of roads had distanced themselves
from each other, tipped up, as over something buried, waking.

       I tripped on them often on that trip, like feeling the bed
       fall away near sleep. In last night's dream we walked again
         down

to bright boats sunk in ruts in the grit. I went down
to gather bits of painted floors slow-ground in the tideless bay;

       you said, Don't, I'd ruin my shoes in that *rubbish*. I did,
       but at least some is with me now: cracked-up, half-rubbed-
         away

pieces of the unfathomable, finally slung
to the beach after the pounding to click in the waves' drag back

       or dry beside the blue hulls, little shards in my apartment.
       I tamper with the clock tonight so that it paddles it in

to me again like a private tide, letting me forget,
for a while, I am forgetting you. The clock cradles

>the hours as the hands spread and clasp and spread across the
>>face
>lined with such a measured breakdown of life. Beside it the
>>framed

scrap of a time, teetering town, lapis and pearly
dream-laced water, arbitrary shoreline binding as it

>separates but the seam hidden or not there at all beyond
>the idea of a place where two things meet and don't become
>>one,

the thought of meeting buried under waves at a point that
doesn't exist beyond the froth rush, mud clouds, and savage

>beating of itself. If the photo were torn along this margin
>between gesticulating, nomad sea and headstrong cliff,

then fitted back together, you wouldn't know the difference.
The line will always spill off, the way the quilt rolls over

>to show a strip of faded lining, the color of a time
>confined to black and white. In the color photo it's the color

left out, receding, crashing back, caught here, and not.

The Divorce

She can't concentrate,
again checks the caged
mice in the classroom.
She counts up to five
and back again, tries

not to cry. The mice
have had pink babies.
Worried Mom and Dad
will eat more children,
she stops learning to

read, drops two reading
levels, reads without
understanding the
words, sees only black
stitches hurrying

across the pages,
follows them, counting,
not reading. Instead
of the Holt reader's
"cookies for the girl,"

numbers on her tongue.
She has learned to count
syllables. These are
understandable.
She knows what follows

each number. She claps
out the syllables
of words in her mind.
Favorites have five;
they fit in her hand.

She pictures herself
as an audience:
everything over
too soon. Not knowing
why, she keeps clapping.

Florida

Alafia, Withlacoochee. Brazilian pepper, melaleuca, Australian pine.
Paper-bubble, lettered-olive, conch, coquina, monkey-tusk bedding with
    teeth

of lemon or bull shark, black in the loss of fifteen million years. Home.
    Blind tendrils
bump and hook the iron knit of a just-placed garden chair. Cadaverous moss
    climbs down.

Stand and you sink in the whiskered ferns, curled with birth. And there *are*
    hills—that don't quite fit
like the cypress knees or lumps in throats. Azaleas gash the low dip of
    wadded

magnolias like a crack in a word thought calm. Slow water, thick wind—but
    inland
among the little Etrurias, Rosewoods, cracked parking lots, something
    swells the flat.

Dirt's attempt at tears? Hot weeds bent above overturned bowls, giant
    ghoul-bellies of brim.
Who accounts for the spilled, swallowed, for me contained, spilled? A
    finger hung

in the warm water, slit on sword grass or buzzing palmetto. Molten noons,
    the swim
on distant pavement, evenings like lizards' neon throats cast full, gone in a
    wave,

and always the heat, even in the foam that won't come in, on waves grime-
    jade
then orange as signs on closed roads, finally black around the long crease of
    moonlight,

mounds both steadfast and shifting: not mine, mine, stung finger
    cooling, always
pointing off where the wilderness of the ocean meets the smaller void
    of the Gulf.

Pavement, Italian

You remembered the corner
of a mosaic floor: tiny green and white

cubes of stone laid to mimic
fallen leaves in a broom-swept heap. You left

the ancient villa, past shops—
tubs of ice and fish, their skin brimming, still,

with moon on breezy inlets;
eyes, the lightless deep. *Plenty still at sea.*

But you walked back to the ruins
and this time noticed the center of that floor:

two more tiled leaves curled there
as if missed by the broom or blown back like thought—

lovely failure, tender mess. Out of place
for all time, the small thing that once touched you.

You told me over and over
as if to make sure I'd remember.

For the Nights of Saint Lawrence

Saint of stained glass, confectioners, Ceylon,
of laundry, comics, libraries, and having

the last word: gridiron dragged to every fresco.
Saint of burning down, of cooks, and saving,

of shooting stars in August when your sun's
a brand on each noon passing like a slow cow.

In the church of San Lorenzo, Bronzino
hasn't chained or strapped you to the grill but lets

your magnificent body lithely lounge
above the flames. You seem about to speak

the words they say you said (pink-wick fingers
flared in pose): *You can turn me over now.*

This side's done. But these books say
the other books are wrong: more the custom,

Lawrence was decapitated, taken
after Pope Sixtus II was beheaded

on the Appian Way in 258
while holding a funeral. When the prefect

demanded the church's treasures, Lawrence
gathered Rome's poor and sick and answered

Here they are—perhaps also unlikely,
like a fervid will beside which fire

is nothing. But what of a story
if it hoists reason over wretched truth,

like tucking black-vined amphoras in tombs,
like those people I've known a few of

who seem to drift in larger time than life has.
Bronzino's stooping fire tenders twist,

nude, except for little kerchiefs forever
slipping from their crotches as they scoop

and haul more tinder to the pyre. One hunk
squats and pumps a bellows at the sparks.

Bronzino's deviation into beauty.
Notion someone really might be watching,

that there is compensation for crucifixion,
that despair gets registered and will be

sanctified. That pain dies soon, though each murder
lasts for thousands and thousands of years.

Some Lines to the Waves

Pink moon jelly, brown-bulbed weed,
and the serial, busted-up lines of nudged lather:
hissing, provisional lace, so white
it's barely there, flaking, lifting, stirring, stirred
with the blank sand, not unlike the tether
of any given moment. You spill out

squat, nose-dashed sand dollars, shin of ship,
glass smoothed unsmooth and foggish, the odd tap
of cowrie, cockle, halved blue mussel.
Now and then the losses tip
into too much. All dents, gleams, you shove up
a collapsed gull with blackened sockets, grassy tassel

of severed something, stink, and the unbound
sun pokes your man-sized mounds of sea palm, oozed
bright. Today, like you, I stop here, slipped-back whisper,
now bemoaning, now imploring explanation, swooned
with pieces of the sky, bruised
from periwinkle, raw with jasper.

Found Photo, Florence in the Background

Here you are like the window of a house
I can't enter. War is more recent,
and the stones haven't yet stood the last flood.
On a hill over town, your brow midway

between cathedral and tower, you gaze
toward the river, but it isn't what you see.
You're looking at something outside
the picture, past the Old Bridge, built-upon

as if bridge alone weren't enough.
Your young feet here point neither up-hill
nor down, already wise to how
direction misleads. Whose kiss pulses

on these sunlit lips? What stockinged girl
traipsed through your thoughts that hazy morning
as you brushed your shoes new for the shot?
You wait, so sleek in this stolen photo,

your gaze abstract, content. No trace of me
in the light off your cheek, pant cuff.
Have you yet mused how a life can change
in the time it takes to kiss the boundaries

of a neck? *Wait there*. Though you seem to,
the past won't be filled by scant now.
I may only fancy that this slip of gray,
this perfection of waiting, is for me.

Robert Capa's Last Photograph

Soldiers advancing through low brush. Not your best.
More a memorization of the grass:

blurred boots raised for the next step. Uncompressed
gray. Not like art, this frame eleven. Buried

in the weeds out there is the mine that kills you,
as if you are about to walk in on

your own trick of picking off the moments
as they cross. A photo of how anyone

might go. So, not news: torn jungle, passage.
The helmet's on your ears another hour

through tense fields of monotonous composition.
Death is still a secret. In the urn

of the camera, a man lies on a road—
armless?—or are they tied? Earlier, same roll,

you'd shot a boy soldier, cheek against
a wooden pillar. His eyes, dreaming, look

farther than seeing. You bowed down before him,
the camera's small black room, a gun of blanks

saving no one. Taking. Years before,
your famous *Death of a Loyalist Militiaman*

catches him but can't as he steps from life.
You snapped it quicker than blood could fill

the bullet's moat. Flown up behind his head, bone
or bullet or life, itself? Repeating

in the museum, in the head. Then China:
little boys thrilled in snow. Packed brilliance

stayed in flight, one head thrown back to trap
the wheeling flakes in his lashes—all

the embroidered sky in laughing eyes
while the others sling their white grenades, lost

in snow wars. They barely know who they are
in this evacuation, false death of play

or work, as if doing were a drill
for how to die. Not even nightmare, this last

photograph's re-reopening on the too-calm,
stubborn waste. Forgettable dreams are the ones

that allow for rest, not thrilled, not bleeding.
A masterpiece paced to regular breath.

That other art of giving one's life.
Men and the wide horizon like the end.

II

Geppetto

The skeleton clicks, always doubling
over in my hands. Damned things that steal soul
and leave. Mine, the son of a virgin father

and a blue-haired elf. No wonder it was hard
for him to be good. No wonder he tried
to flee my life, gibberish script of that drunk

who wrote to pay debts. Poor carver, impotent
creator, I whittled at the giggling branch
of swindler destiny. When my son went,

no whine of new hinged ankles won him back.
Borrow children. They are not ours.
Another spelling book. His burnt feet.

Finding him in the bowels of the old fish
out of which my dear doll lead me onto
the star-stung sea. The legs I honed and taught,

they always ran ahead. The same thing that saves
the heart breaks it. Now he's real. Only
the stub of one genuine nose remains.

The begged, the lost, the made: my life scrawled
and hocked by that drunk debtor who knew
we're all born unreal. Knew about miracle.

Landscape, American

Smudged garage from which metallic screams fly up.
Asphalt like too much makeup (the swamp bucks

when it pours). But cars keep coming over the convex,
crimped tar bound by strip malls. Boomtown. Womanized

woman or man. Vacant lots loiter with weeds
and corroded, brown bed springs like pans of turkey

picked clean. Buildings' stumps squat in the sun, homeless,
steps climbing no place. Can air be depicted?

July's here is snail skin and sunburn stuck back
in the sun. Dead oil holes wheeze up from Lethe.

But through the Stygian humidity, crape myrtles frill
and the oaks plow up my mildewed mailbox as it seals

off evidence of everywhere else. Poor town, conceived
in the heat of some version of passion like us.

Son of Medea

Sunlight sang through the thick door's crack.
      And I heard her words,
            yet chose not to wake my brother,

the one content to toss his ball
      eternally. Sad
            is what they called me, wandering

the streets far as I was allowed,
      and then I would go
            one more. Both mother and father,

but more mother, dark of eye, hand.
      My face hers, they said.
            Unworried, forgetful brother,

sleep on. Your death is dead. Mine spreads,
      ravels like spring clouds.
            Mother/father, sky/field, wave/rock,

when will men see how unions are
      impossible, birth
            proof of nothing, no link of life.

Small likeness, but hollow. Circle
      around the failure
            to incarnate. Imaginings

can't agree with flesh. Father went.
      How could we have lived?
            Invalid promises. He'd bring

toys: stuffed, golden lambs of wool-scrap
          sewn to suck at love,
                    kiss-worn, stitch-lip feigning, teaching

what it is to love—fleece borne to
          hearth fire. We're the scorch
                    of dislodged bones, the joint dissolved.

Mother, Father survive, wither,
          wander. Forever
                    children, we live in death's black nut,

gardens at night. No ichor here.
          I'm gift gown, burnt crown,
                    wrath's volume, passion's girth. Canyons

for a gut, a child of divorce,
          a grave. But the clouds—
                    I waved arms I could not move. Wisps

of shaggy cirrus couched our craft.
          As if drowsed, I strained
                    to admire the jade sun-dragons,

the approving blue of the sky,
          to sit up, reach for
                    those splendid serpents! Mother's arm

cradled my small back; I could not
          feel it there. Pretty,
                    feathery sun ram—yes, my death

was radiant—dazzling spiral
          of horns, you came late.
                    Now I'm alone. The beguiling

symbols gone. I am no longer
        damned as their love. Freed
                from belief in what cannot be.

Chameleons at the Window

Chameleons sleep on the frame's warm remove
around the midday window. Hours, they hang
by bulbed, Martian toes in the chipped, shady groove
with closed-bud eyes. Now their colors belong

to the twig traceries of leaf-stained sun fall.
But instead of the breezy, arabesque spreads
of bunched green, they prefer old paint on wood, loll
all day on cracked blue, dusty glass at their heads.

One wakes, turns with an unlizardly smooth lift
of chin while darkening to speckled black-browns—
still nothing close to blue. On my chair I shift,
knowing the lure of impossible backgrounds.

The hot pane slides down. The chameleons fly
in their dreams of blue. Smudges on hard sky.

Drafts for a Double Sonnet

#1 The Cobbler

In his shop by the arch, your cobbler
wouldn't give a definite when,
wrote your name on the sole of my loafer,
said, Just come back when you can.

But I was leaving you—
the entire country. I would pack
with or without that shoe.
This time try not to come back.

Finished, —just in time of course—
he even shined the pair of them for me,
so I wore them the last hours
we walked the stones in that revelry

of heels tricked on corrosion, night heat,
wine, lamplight I've only known with . . . . You
stopped, wiped away the street
with your hand, said, nothing to do

about distance, mortgage, career,
ink seas of Italian.
The turn for me, you couldn't steer
or wouldn't. There were things to be done

at home. I left still loving. Such
a long way after, today, I saw that crimped line
under my shoe and how the damned arch
of the sole holds, with all the force of its design,

your name, safe from all my stamping.

#2 The Rite

If only to consume the memory, upturn
that bend of brain where memories keep
like rock in hills—I take you up,
an ice thing, to thaw the bluish brown
to something redder. It never suffices
to only drain the hard away, restore
the tender: I light the oven, smear
the garlic, the pepper-grit of spices.

Do I savor the formal, tragic sips?
No. It's a bland and every-day affair.
Preparing it I forget you are
this flank crossed out with lines of char.
It's just my rite when waves of your soft hair
become the black napkin I bring to my lips.

#3 Double Sonnet, Failed

While I'm falling into sleep, across
the ocean you are climbing out. Heavily
soaked in sleep, you mumble of some loss,
eyes closed. My theory is we're bound, every
now and then, to pass each other. We are
traveling the same road, you gazing
into one direction, I the other. So far
there's been no moment of this near-grazing
before the gap between us widens once
again. I've waited for it like an eclipse
of two outer, unlit planets. Days, months
don't exist there, nor light and dark unclasp

when it's over, an eclipse in total darkness.
We know that dreams cannot touch but maybe
sleepers can, pure in their forgetfulness,
brush as if traversing a dim lobby
or any place not a destination. Awake
we once did pass on Viale Volta, down
where it crosses the periphery to take
you up the hills above, out of town—
we walked our antipodal courses even then,
you on the other side of flint-hot
Volta, waving out a match. Even then
we walked so like strangers, I almost did not
  call to you. These nights I search with doubt,
  call into myself for you, not out.

On Work

I. Song of the Locksmith

Imagine an island's ragged coast at night or a city skyline
wound round inside an infant's nostril. Call me diplomat,

fisherman, miracle faker, stir-jiggling out the shapes of shock
with tines of ruined forks. I prod oiled midnights without dissolving

in the geode of dream. I'm key across mashed spoons, shredded tin,
my box of lures jammed with splintered wedges, a shower

of hair pins, scuffed zip-lock of sesame seeds for luck. Call me
shrink to your physical slip-ups. Say each lock's another lover.

But after the rhyme of notched metals yielding up their glistening
thickets, the sigh and whine, the abstracted swing—in that breeze

from another's rooms—I don't cross through. Residents reclaim,
pay, and I'm outside, alone, off to bicker with more mouse-mouths,

trick another spring and hope, again, that it just happens
as after the clearing of the mind. What if thought did not slide back,

the deepest tooth twisting into the nerve to clench the hinge
forever. How easily I could step into another life

of entering, make more money. But I'm a man of compromise;
I work the system, which is still better than you watching,

impatient for the cage, snatched from the undertow of *these things
happen*. One of your lives wasted, you step back through.

II. Pickpocket's Piece

The bus has its regulars: the woman on her way to her lover's
spreading oil into the rumpled linen of her lips before the lipstick;

the Chinese poet peering, then writing delicate insects down the page.
We let each other be; they understand that owning isn't forever.

I fuse into the giddy cloud of tourists, into the pressed affection
of the newly-weds in each other's pockets or sink my wrist

in the abyss of her red bag. Round us, laughter, whooping windows
and the bus' own sluggish drawl as it pushes up the tilted fields

of silver olives. Heart beat buried in the engine's syncopation,
I slash the sun from the branching dusk like a prize citron as I catch

the vertiginous off-rhyme of a change pouch yapping in my fingers.
Sure, there'll be the stuff I didn't want: unmarked pills, tissues

damp with colds or crying. Number of someone's perspective lover,
notes scrawled in dank cathedrals, gritty mints, the crap that nestles

with loose thread, depressing disorder like the messiness in the head.
Like touching something frozen and feeling it burn. Your soul

or just your money, the bits sticking which-ways through my fingers,
a cross-stitch between your pocket and mine. Who has the right to

anything but his flesh? Why isn't flesh enough? I press at it
and merely enter pockets. What do you have to lose?

Losing My Italian

The hall chair in Via del Castagno,
chair that had become *la sedia* through
and through, completely *sedia*, now is
ebbing back to chair. I cannot recall

the exact intensity of the poppies
puddling the May fields along the train's route
toward Arezzo and all the crumbling,
repair, and crumbling. I miss less and less

slender lanes and cold black thresholds leading
on to blinding courtyards garnished with basil,
the chatter of forks on dishes overhead,
tipsy afternoons, the heaping sugars

in my coffee. Sometimes I awake
in a trench of night, my mouth full of pieces
of the overused, eternal questions.
Other nights it has completely left me,

my tongue an empty drawer. Finally sleeping
I climb the ruined hotel that hangs
along cliffs. Steps compose themselves from sand
and I walk up. I want to call—

but when my Italian goes, vowels melt
into one another. Then I believe
I hear things from the box of smeared letters,
a murmur in the harsh remote. Italian

movies aren't even helping. They only stroke it
for a while. The southern accents, after
the undressing and caressing, leave by
morning. The gleam is hard to look at. A dream

has taken something with it. Not tragic;
I can't keep everything. Only the smash
of the glossed *portone* in its jamb.
The hot stones piecing themselves to the station.

The lit dust on stems of sage takes its place
like any *terra* beneath the plane that climbs
the dear, defiant, unbearable path
into wind and out of articulation.

Three Minutes

My friend asked why I set my watch ahead.
        But certain things are done in that
                vacuum tunneling

into the body so that you breathe. Instead
        of trying to stop time, I strive
                for ellipsis,

air-holes in the lid over the hostage crickets;
        room where the smell of fried peppers
                slipped in and held

before carrying on to where time goes
        in its neither becoming
                the river nor coming

back with the smell of rain: stairwell, August
        1989; novel yellowed
                in June of '95;

you holding a book, drifting off—did your thumbs
        float at the margins? Did a palm
                press the spine?

The pieces I possess are everything
        I lack. Wound to my wrist with time's
                spangled cosmos

obliterated by the day, these three minutes,
        like the sweet spills approaching rest,
                lend something more.

Hour Between Bird and Bat

In the beryl glow a bat fell for a bird,
and the town went under like an island,
still full of the day as dream is with life.

Petals shone like beached pebbles ablaze where
the tide still touches. Light leaned to shadow
then was shadow itself. The soarers' song

thrilled off the branches like leaves in October
and struck the bat's beam, lit there, so that she
would get up earlier tomorrow. All

night she yanked at mountainous horizons,
heart scratching across the screen. This is how
the Alps pantomimed towers. Hill, cypress:

dome, belfry. In the lilting gusts the bat
was dream dropped awake, full of bells, the mint
on the breeze, tint in blindness. Salami

sandwiches and hunger. Anything seemed
possible. Below, a manic slob fell
in fiery love with a charming starlet.

A black bowl broke. A moment could nearly
be pieced back to time, the edges meeting,
if merely, less than meeting between.

Morning at Ocean Beach

I walk to the bus past the Six A.M. Bar,
fog putting out the pinks, blues, greens, and start
to grasp how you've joined the throng of my distractions,
fists of exhaust opening to the street

of exhausted mornings, dissembling into
the weather like spirits or memories
of your face. I walk the beach holding thoughts
of you between tooth and lip, and there is

the Pacific, frothed with its own unpeaceful
visions which it saves, half-drowned, in erasures
on the brows of the waves. But I want the blue
you never reach when you dive in it.

When the tide comes in like another form
of darkness and rubs the beach away, I want
that flood of cold oblivions. I don't
want a love poem; I want back what the waves

have taken down slowly in over-full mouths.
I don't want to write it . . . . This is how
you drizzle intervals of dreaming here
over woken mornings like flower boxes

streaking the windows of the bus with buds
the fuchsia of an afternoon in bed.
And as with pricks of recollection during
great punctuations of distance and months,

white flowers burn in the dangles of dark vines.
Distraction, I don't want to go home, don't
want to write or pull at tousled laundry,
the sear, pop and crumple of desire; I want

just *desire*. Not the letters of the word.
I don't want to be alone. It's midnight
in the heart when you've kept your hands like this,
here inside my clothes, though your hands are far

away. I retrace the shoreline, spend the day
at the tides museum where nothing's said
of the blue, just more about the sameness
of the change. Too much is kept from us.

In the pictures the moon pulls at the water.
I scribble *orbit, salt-crash, thirst*. Out there
waves take down the castles. You are not mine,
not here, where the sky's white, wild and fearless

of falling too far. The sun doesn't rise here
from the ocean, but just before light strikes the waves,
they glow—gas-blue, jade, fire at once—between
quivering sheets of foam, through the wordless fog.

Last Trip to Florida

Wind kept tipping over the pot of red
poinsettia outside your sealed house.
Three days I stooped and stood it up again
and learned about the chambers of the heart

in slick pamphlets with the organs sketched: striped
aortas, hearts like shrunken, eyeless heads.
My flight left after the surgery so all
that happened next happened far away,

clouds between us, punched black-green where the Gulf
gently rocks the rips of foam back in.
They glare and fade like angry ghosts. Here
only every now and then I think

about you and those days I pinched up
the soil before it blended back to dirt,
think of machines that breathe, blood gas, strokes,
and you unlearning to talk. As they split

your sternum, the t.v. panned wrecked roads.
Nurses said you'd sleep all day. You're still asleep,
perhaps will always be. I list things
you showed me: rummy, how to crack pecans,

carve spoons from sticks off the sour orange, melt candles
to make them stand, wrap dimes into vein-blue logs
for my college fund, form a fist . . . all you
poems that have got to come out, enough. Go.

The Tree Where Pinocchio Was Hanged

If you take the elm-lined road or even the grassier paths
that swoop at the river past the small, poetic monuments
taming this end of the Cascine (the fountain of Narcissus,

the pyramid where winter ice was stored away for summer)
and go beyond the Peacock House, an immense field opens:

place where nothing much occurred in real life. Where the innocent,
wooden liar who didn't exist wasn't strung up by masked
assassins. The story the milder twin to the world of things

that do happen but aren't written in stone or books. The tree
did dominate the "Field of the Big Oak" until last century

when it died of old age. Ascension Day, crickets are sold
in beribboned wicker cages here. And the weeds speed on
along the river as if also on their way to Pisa and the sea.

At the farthest green tip, just before park frays into concrete,
tracks and suburbs, the tomb of an Indian prince stands canopied

at the point where two rivers flow together. Handsome bust
in rust-red marble, he'd fallen ill while visiting Florence.
It's said the depths of the park leading to his grave are overrun

by elves mottled like the plane trees and like the intangible coinage
of shade from their lurching leaves, brief dapples where two parks

wrestle with each other, body, soul, like the two rivers, oak
that was with the puppet who wasn't. Fire eaters, peacocks,
prostitutes and drugs. Was it his own beauty that gripped Narcissus—

or that of the other, unreal one gazing up from the place
where nothing real happens—when he changed into flowers?

Matera

Three Matera's: one glass; one bone-beige
chiseled from stone; and finally the one of caves
where lizards flashed like dream loosed on sleep.

I have a picture of you in it, of it:
sweater, hair and rock, the same blond ash
as if you risked dissolving in that sand

abandonment and noon of early spring,
no life there but wild dogs and lichen
and the hinges that groaned like a river would

devouring chunks of its bank. Town sliced
like time while geography turned its head.
We were twenty. Ripping raw peppers, bread,

we sat on a brink. Lemony petals bobbed
from rose erosion. A horseshoe dribbled
brown luck down the front of a burrowed chapel,

stains more like notes of other musics. When
I kicked a stone through a doorless door, that boy
on his battered bike creaked by, bleating a song

we couldn't understand. Out came the dogs,
and we rushed back to the square of gathered men.
Time stretched before us. A page of me blew away.

When the Crucifix Spoke to Francis

Maybe it was the cold stone, its universe

       transposing the knees,
a dreaming in a nerve tassel. But maybe
       somebody's God did

ply the figured lips, crash frown to spreading
       robins. Words spurt
from ossifying wood: *My house is falling down*

       and this bent man
the one to reconstruct it without brick brocades
       of his father's wealth,

each silk a guilt to shed on the raw piazza,
       peels of stunning tints
to drop to cracking hands. Silence now. The mouth

       refreezing, dull
as a remote star, the gaze reentering paint.
       But Francis shook—

had he prayed too long, gray-kneed, smoke-eyed? He'd seen
       wrong, yet it spoke
or didn't. Fingers numb on his hugging fists

       (and it only gets colder),
in the taper-dark, faith flattened like a beast
       giving way: wolf

smoothed to dog; decision to stay out there until
       the birds would come down
to a vulgar tongue in praise. Burlap roped to

little time. Did he
hear the voice again? Did rock truly shift its jaws
in groans of mercy

when the demon tried to fling him from the cliff?
And if it was
just the frozen earth all along that nailed at

his palms? That loved him
in its cruel and earthly way. And the moon.
And the flowers

bled for pictures: a splintered child insisting
Repair My House.
The decision to know that he had heard.

Front Page, *International Herald Tribune*, 11 September 2001

Coming across it in the piles and piles
of papers since. Ice and warmth at once:
blown-up, lovely anemone clown fish
gazing at the camera from a garden glade
of Great Barrier Reef coral I read
is "under assault." Doll-like lips and dark,
dark eyes. Enormous ruffle-fins around
its cheeks, body brightly banded. To think
of the clear morning indulging itself
in furry-fingered coral and the wide-eyed
eloquence of fish. So velvety a scene
I try to touch it. Then below, a "Bitter Feud
Over Gucci" beside "Once Nearly Extinct,
Jewish Communities Are Reborn in Germany";
a shot of Oki-ni's Nile-carp-skin sneakers.
I can't bring myself to put it down,

gray crumpling heft more vital than a book.
Weeks ago someone said to me, Now we know
what it's like to feel the horror felt each day
around the world. I think I nodded yes,
as if even this might be another brand
of privilege: knowing how it is when everything
turns to newspaper, how office desks can blast
into bedrooms down the street, to finally
know what it's like to feel the indecency
of words, the selfish, impotent, perverted
affirmations of a poem. Saints
of burning down, of having the last word,
of having nothing. I pile the papers
over this one from that dreaming morning,
go out into the non-poetic street,
leave living free of poetry a while.

III

To a Movie Star

You drive through the Western town of my desire.
The thirst-hinged dusty sign swings and sings. I can
not believe you pitched those millions from the train,
but I can smell that hotel, feel the vinyl furniture
on my thighs, let the sweat on the ice bucket flare
against my wrist and start to slide. For God's sake take
that woman to bed so I can watch her tongue strike
a brush fire down your chest. The beatings you bear

for us; the hard love you make like a difficult
bed, heaving, smoothing, leaving here another
gift: the open-bloomed bed of dream, my own skin,
and mornings engrossed in the ceiling. Unwrecked.
Free. Kiss the back of my neck in bed some more
as I cross the littered boulevard in the sun.

Arachne

Their moral for my ruin: don't compete
with gods. But where's the sin in excellence?
They are petty. Mine was art. Arrogance?
Naturally. But within the mortal net
of my hands, the world breathed. I wove the truth
(you should, too, though They blast us each to bug).
Beside me Minerva laced her woof with wrath,
tinseled pretty gods, herself, her green drug
of olives. Into her whorled corners she tucked
warnings: proud girls feathered, fanged or packed

in trees, framed all with silver-banded
lies of olive leaves. Instead I wrought
in wool those crimes of gods that I could fit
upon the tract of my loom: Europa stranded
on the fraud of Jove's bull-back in high sea,
her terror brimming, silken; Leda gagged
by plumes, ripped, plunging. The abraded thigh . . .
Assembling thread and testament, I tugged
the wreckage into bold, twilled ridges,
piling it like rock strata through the ages.

My weave lacked only tales of justice: hard
for me; I knew none. I was poor, did my best.
My shuttle choreographed color, wrist
racing, the work's weight lifting like a huge bird
for the hour—*this* is my divinity
(for heaven's just reflections off the Earth).
Having lost, Minerva slashed my tapestry,
beat me with her shuttle. Brave, beneath
my ceiling beams I hitched a frazzled strap
as to a new loom, looped a hole to drop

my life into before she touched that, too.
But as I sank and broke, she raised me out
of death, of life, threw me down between, wet
with poison that sucked my tongue to stinger, blew
my belly round, hairy, drizzled fingers to legs
small as stitches. A pale ray drooled off
my awful head in the colorless flags
of no human country, clingy tangles, half
thought, half inner buzz. I sought propped brooms,
the underneath, the barrens of dust in sealed rooms.

As for that third weaver who strung all Their wrongs
into one song—what I'd have done!—I face
it for you, Ovid. Through me you laundered voice
and fault. "A senseless lust for glory" hangs
me here. And you? Weren't our complaints the same?
So I, too, wind my corded codes, though cast
in witch hair, hackneyed scrims that parody dim
heaven. But in the morning when soused
by Apollo's sweating horses as they strain
up the canyon of the sky, my dull knots shine.

And my fate is mine. I am its author
and blight. Each predestined trap I tip's my own.
I'm maker, not inheritor, not bastard spawn
of Jove. Unblessed, I toiled the feather
into my fingers' spirit, bore the snap
and burn of the bones in the back of my hand.
Beast—yet less beastly than They—I hitch a warp
of will to a jamb. Wads of my slain craft unwind
toward chandeliers, I fashion constellations, rig
my own heaven, spit my throne on my silver rug.

I have crept near old immigrant ladies
alone in their strange languages crocheting
trunks of lace, the click of needles weighing
each twist, each ring around the missing: daisies
burst on absent meadows, more a smoke
of vacancy than thread, chinks the size of the stone
that enters the shoe. I taught them how to trick
loss by latticing the day. And I've been
grimy in the factories of their daughters,
in the roar and ache, near hands flattening tatters

on steel plates. I'm there with anyone who makes.
Then on vaults of Italian churches, I fly
with the frescoed angels, shadow the trompe l'oeil
of dangled feet. Each renaissance takes
from me a new draft of perspective: I wove
in Emerson's room. His fist cleared me out
each dawn. He watched my abysmal drops, my drive,
admired how I tilted, eyed the void, and shot.
Then he sat to write with that moon, pearl gristle
snarled, shrunk and waving on his knuckle.

Now I anchor in the echoes of woof and warp
on the cool ribs of radiators in June.
Mostly unobserved, I turn and pull a line
to x-ray, rage caught in a corner's rut, a rope
up to memory that now and then sways, curled,
on the ceiling. Sloughed skins of dream or prayer,
patch where the door last slammed on another world,
sketched brokenness, maps into diamonds, the sheer
sheen of kimonos—this relentless spider heart:
eternity's akimbo. Exile. Art.

One Evening

when I was four the neighbors' dog
     was limping so

I found her screwed-off paw
     tucked in the lawn

between the houses. Her feet
     were all quickly

accounted for, and it was clear
     that I'd found

a dead bat. In the dark I
     hadn't noticed

the gray pages of flesh folded
     with something like

toothpicks inside. Hair more like mine.
     The small bat seemed

ungrown yet was already gone.
     The damp clod gleamed

in the lamplight off the porches.
     I didn't know

how to put it down, the cold
     winged paw. Mine.

Grapefruit

From the chair where you're tied, far
from here, you yell at me, *Bring it back!*
A thing there and not, and we have something
in common as in the old grapefruit days

in winter when I chose fallen ones sunk low
in the grass where they rolled,
gold eggs. Before the snap in the sky,
the crash, they floated atop crowds of leaves

that nuzzled, licked them all their lives
and tossed them out and back again.
I cupped each in moist, feathery fingers,
brought them to you down on a knee,

one foot flat, pressing balance.
You'd hold one of those cooled balls of morning
in a single thick palm, unfold knife, slide it in
to cut the spraying conic, then squeeze

till streams streaked the pale, dusty peel.
Taste of rage and relief. So long ago.
From a green, windy suspension
I'll bring it back, the bright moon, cocoon.

Press the blade through the cottony rind,
through the clouds. Look: the rivers of bitterness
and gold, the velvet shades of flight.
You take them now.

Crown for *Piazza della Santissima Annunziata*

The porticos tether a gray hem of heaven.
The ragged paving stones crest and dip
so that one trips—eons of this mean slap
they call culture. I've crossed in every season,
in all states of mind. Not home, though a person
can't help but try. One crook of the stonescape
doesn't release itself into streets: a trap
of buildings walls the way as angles open

to clouds. But it's always new like an ocean's shore.
Today the stone is soaked with rain like sand
when the tide's just out. They say *spiazzare*—confuse:
rip you from this piazza, drop you elsewhere.
Fountains, miracle, orphanage. Harmony and
dissolution in a sandstone crib of breeze.

*

Serena's the stone of dissolution. Its storm-blue
surface dwindles like wind-shorn sandcastles.
Perhaps the fountains aren't strange here: puckered muzzles
of spitting sea imps; a tangled, lazy spew
from nozzled gills and mollusks; nightmare's fish stew
for surf-starved Florence. A drizzle jostles
into cupped flukes hoisted in the slipknot-pretzels
of finned tentacles, toes—or tails? Inland sea-show

of poised chaos and webbed border beasts dragged back
from where the sea roils off into the depths of the stars,
making fun, if not sense, of freakish grace.
Oceanic cherubs spritz the catfish-dragons' thick-
er spouts that climb more sluggishly, and the green bronze stirs
as with longing for some uncast, looser bliss.

                         *

As with longing, the statue of the Grand Duke
on horseback advances in his frozen
way toward the Way of the Servants (of Mary). Brazen
stance, leading the way, and with that quake
in his expression as he turns a fiery look
up at his lover's window. Such mild treason,
this bronze-stopped glance. To his right a soup kitchen
draws drunks who crouch about the steps. Horse, boot, cheek,

all of the statue, recast from Turkish cannons.
This was the Duke to found Livorno on the coast—
hence that pair of fishy fountains flanking him;
originals, in Livorno, drown in sea winds
while our lily valley copies burn like lust,
spray parched at once on each scaly arm.

                         *

Above the spray, dry scales, and blazing gaze,
rounds of terracotta ground the flying arches
of the old orphanage. Each spandrel couches
a scantly bundled baby circled by blue glaze
as if the babies rise in perfect skies.
Named for the Innocents, the place touches
on how scores died so He might live. Each watches
as I cross the piazza, inquisitive eyes

above swaddled feet musing on my every step.
Beneath, a stone marks where for centuries a wheel—
lazy-Susan style, half-outside, half-in—
anonymously swiveled in mishap
infants in the night. Somewhere a muffled bell
tolled each turn to rouse a dozing nun.

                              *

Bells toll and nuns turn into the church for mass
where black-gold-black baroque suggests a succession
of colossal caskets nailed outside-in.
In Sicily a giant, white-lace bride's dress
would smother these naves and asps; the cake's mess
of icing would stucco the vaults. So much sun . . .
But in here, in the dark, sight does return
enough to find the silver *voti* hung like moss

around the miraculous *Annunciation*
where the timid artist, having done the rest,
lay down to nap before he dared Her face.
While he slept, an angel's pity—exasperation?—
bloomed into the blank this brow both blessed and lost,
eyes flooded with dawning and abyss.

                              *

In this valley of art and flood, everything
blisters and fades as in the glassed cloister
leading back outside. Here torrid heat and moister
winters blanch the still-green robe that Rosso slung
so it would slip clean off his fresco like a wing
slicing through that air into this of moldered plaster.
His mob have thrown back their heads in a fluster
as cherubim buoy Mary above the throng.

Next, Pontormo's Elizabeth is accosted
by the Virgin before this *same* church's square.
A nude boy on the steps examines his outer thigh,
and in the crowd two women and a strong-wristed
blond man sketching—it's you, Pontormo!—stare,
not at *The Visitation*, but at me

                          *

and it occurs to me that *visitation*
to Pontormo meant the body's visit to
the spirit: the naked, ample shoulder's throw
of muscle, neck balancing sack, the exertion
of kneeling calves. The formless spirit's ration
are these forms. Outside, that always new
light's being laid on the old piazza as though
even days are orphaned with Earth's each rotation.

Duke, painter, orphans and the miracle
of another ambivalent mother
filling with the all, the lack. Cumbrous bubble,
doubling distance. The fish-eyed peduncle
floating between seas and stars and neither.
Heaven. Porticos hefting the gray ravel.

The Ocean, Not the Sea

Here there is the sea but not the ocean,
not shapelessness, no
scrubbed piles of gulping shells caught
in the sleek weed torn from never-surfacing hillsides:

just tideless here. Slug of the Mediterranean.
Its cliffs are chiseled to shelves
of book-like villas.
Beaches: flapping orchards of umbrellas—

such straight lines up and down the crooked shore.
The far ocean's crash
(blue as the night-painted vaults
in Siena) dies on the distances. The sky is

the only relief—though, since when does the sky relieve.
Instead, this mothery well's
whispers echo, walled
by land that, itself, is walled wallessly

by oceans' everything. Even the Grand
Canal forgets what
vastness the possible needs,
room there also for impossible, the mind shoved off

from its chattery edge. Once I watched a crazy man
curse the dreadful Pacific
from a wind-thrashed dune.
His flying fists. And that cold god beneath.

Arguing in Italian

All argument could be in Italian:
knowing how to eat well though your blood
may be curdling in defeat. Learning to fully
love beauty, its smells of rot and restoration
clenched in combat, rolling round the corridors.
In New York no one believes the grid of streets
succeeds in holding down confusion lush

as gardens in the tropics while underworlds
and paradises twine side by side through sparkling
or putrid labyrinths of bliss and much, much less.
Such are the complications of Italian.
In it, to merely *think* churns-up a gale
of exacting, choppy grammar, and anything
you *would like* drifts farther than in English,

tangling in sunflower fields of *r's* and *s's*.
—But what glory to learn to slip, unanxious,
into the formal, indeed, to thrash about in it,
when you must . . . . Not to say that life like this
is better or worse than another. But if only
(which only takes one word to say in the voluptuous
yet economical landscape of Italian), if only

all misunderstanding—all words—could be shot
into the ringing, dome-distracted night
like the firework displays on Saint John's Day
when people line the Arno in great hoards
to let the bombs tear straight down through their ears
to nearly cave the heart once more, then watch
the deadly fire turned inside-out again

and again, diving off the hills to freeze
as massive melon flowers that just as fast go out
in gray ghosts that dally a while in front of the stars.
Life should be *this* argument—which is best:
the bright conflagrations, themselves, or the wash
they throw like salt on icy streets against
the facades and faces of the people: all

the city, a stony model, one hundred
dresses, one after another: the riches
of times of peace, mounds of ice cream beyond
what can be eaten. If only we could explode
brilliantly, then take a walk, arm in arm,
perhaps, reach a shrugging compromise, a sort
of peace, over linen doilies and espresso.

Postscript, Beauty

He's dragged the jewel-horned mirrors back in place,
a nausea of gold florescences
convolving, one upon the other. He
won't sit with me at dinner anymore,

bored Adonis, petaled lips pink as pig,
tiny, testy ears of filigreed brooches.
I yawn against his smooth, vanilla neck.
He used to cough to chase away the snarling

in his throat. Now he puts on softer collars,
uncleft spats and believes it is enough.
I've lost him to the easy reflection
of silver bowls. Last night I joked, called him

Beauty; he broke my nose. His heart has dripped
to cold fat while I dream of his lost lips of rams.
What delight we once knew in the walled gardens,
unmanned halls, festoons always rebudding.

The spell's now dust. "Marriage," say my sisters.
We now need fantasies. Before, we were
the most original pair. He took me
to the forests in my bed, his hoofs scrubbing heat

into my archways, the bull calves like the rocks
that break from hills, the stampede in his chest . . . .
I miss the weasel tongue amidst the pins
of his muzzle, how black irises inked

the whole orbs, and a tusk fished me softly out.
Snout like a weather in my hair. Briars
took my insides over. I'm lost. The torn
dog and beetle on his breath weren't foul

as his bisque ringlets at last night's late return.
If I had been the beast, would desire
have rocked him down my bearded belly—
he who swapped the mask of God for mere angel skin—

would he have come near? Beside the dying beast,
I grew more than beautiful. The candy
of my gut distilled to rum as his many-
embered core drowned in perfumes. Glorious

is tragedy in retrospect. He used to see
in the dark, had other sight: we all lock up
a wilderness he showed me, and I would pass time
at the well, at one with wishing in the velvet slime

of the believer. Now I can't wait for my own face
to fold into the unmarked ranges on the globe,
the tilled flesh around the eyes of hags where
form is awful. Beauty enters there. Strange

we strain to name the skin of things. Blinding
eyes slide truth behind the portraits. Now all this
unprincipled symmetry. His shins no longer
shine with wire hair churning into feathers

at the fetlock . . . . This morning he is sorry but
won't come in. Foot toward window, eyes in the fire,
I slip into the rushes. My name was Beauty.
I've immigrated in. I reckon with the truth.

Recuperation at Corpus Christi

I pass Needville on the way, the edge
of the freeway jumbled in trash
and scatters of blue—yellow—white marbles:
Lady Bird's wildflowers between broken
billboards wet, toppling, and stuck on the world.
Tear-eaten tissues from a bad love.

The road to the beach is like waiting for love
in a fast train, at the window's edge,
vision smeared against the world,
hung clothes filling in wind and the trash
sprawled like unbuttoned shirts, broken
wrappers of dreams-come-true, marbles

shot too near the gutter. The surf marbles
with foam that barely shifts, like love.
Butterflies tear in the wet sand, broken
wings stuck, flattening on the edge
where the Gulf comes up, prismatic trash.
I'm walking on the lips of the world

where real laps the dream. Nowhere in the world
do you feel so alone. Eyes, like marbles,
blur to look through, can just discern trash
and jellyfish somehow blown-up like love
to ink-balloons, drying at the hazy edge
of shell beds. You always chose the broken

shells. Convicts cleaning the beach have broken
the sand, and one blue bubble-world
of a jellyfish has been popped by the edge
of a boot. Now more popping like marbles
dropped in jars: the prisoners who love
dealing such blows, clothed on the beach, just trash

to pick up. I know how it is when all is trash.
The surf is slick, and the waves have broken
themselves calm, resting now like after love.
We have got to give up on the world,
not fill with wind to dark marbles
quivering on the sand, drowning at the edge.

But all is trash when removed from the edge.
Broken shells we think will gleam like marbles
don't, like love when it visits the world.

Corleto

Corleto Perticara—
how could someone sad as you have been born there?
A happy heart for you, my dear.

It took you years to tell me
of how a lord loved a lady who was living there,
in Corleto Perticara,

when it was just a nameless land.
He wrote her letters in a violent hand and named her town
A Happy Heart for You, My Dear

which over years and tongues wore down
to what these days probably sounds something like
"Hap-hart For-thee-der" to the Italians.

But think how the name must have convinced her
she was welcome on the Earth,
finally welcome in a place whose heart was hers.

You once made me feel that way, that year
you conjugated *love*, replaced *the sky* with *il cielo*,
even laughed. But now I find no map that shows Corleto
and wonder was there ever a happy heart for you, my dear.

Tyrrhenian

Odd moments deliver one fully into
life that's always straying. Fleecy stars

      off the poplars swim
      blindly through the streets

as elements swap properties and even
the spirit might dream itself elemental,

      floating just above,
      already pushing off

like so many ships that didn't come back.
Yesterday I made my way into the sea.

      First time in years. Crowds
      of Italians. It wasn't

the Gulf where I used to go, but in the waves'
rough play lifting me off the drowned sand,

      was it the grief in bliss
      or just the kindred salt

that drew forth the tears? Cold sea against
the bloodstream like a second life,

      the one that lives while I,
      sealed away, manage

to get a few things done. As if shreds
of life (I could say death, but I won't)

sometimes come home.
A fine spit of foam

gleamed on a blurring, gray surge. I was
seven-years-old falling backward into the waves.

Indelible, devastating joy.
The eternity in my lost life.

Landscape, Kimono

On her pocket: purls of vine and yellow stars.
At the collar a comet of zinnias

which repeats on one violet cuff.
The folds—black shafts round her elbow—

lean, deepen like drying canvases dimming
from afternoon into evening.

Between her fingers, some Monte
di Splendore can be glimpsed on her belly

above the poppies in a valley.
On a nearer hill, one plumped with breast,

a lady is departing from the landscape.
All who look on: the busy society

of wastelands in bloom, ruddy buds
beginning as she turns, leaves the room.

Sunbath Rhapsody

The beach is what heaven has to be: double
baptism of the sky
       and the planet. Self turning color, finally

different. I lay myself out, shameless,
to burn a little more
       while the wind waters at the sweat on my stomach,

skin sore where the world's had its way with me,
sand clinging. Touched
       all over without having to be touched.

Then the sea-slash and cold undertow's pull,
dashing neck, dribbling
       into the ears, swallowing the sun. Paradise

of drifting in and out of the day, laid out
like a body with the life
       already gone, reminding me I'm only

alive: eyelids, red embers.

Shipwreck

Tonight woken by the wind, I went out
to lift the pot of sage and the thyme that died
off the risky wall, out of the gusts.

It was warmer than I'd thought, and for the first
time in my life, I saw that it is no
exaggeration when they say *moonlight*

you could read by: cold, gray, but defining
nonetheless, the way a death can dazzle you,
for a few weeks, with the shock of life.

Outside, inside the cold, with the hard, warm wind,
the houses all around were black, shut.
My worst fear, when I was small, at night,

was that I be the only one awake
in all the world. After thinking myself
foolish all these years, I see now

that I was right to be afraid, awake
upon my life like rumpled seas, the only
one awake inside my life. With the hours

until the blue-faced morning washes in.

Smoke

I probably wouldn't have thought of it
but for the little fires people have been tending
in so many blackened circles on the hills
burning the old growth, severed limbs of olives
weakly waving as the orange gashes smoke
the icy air and burn the eyes. The first house
I remember burned down the first December
my father had moved out. Not a tragedy,
though I tend to confuse time with meaning,
as with the turnings of the year, old arm chairs
let go from windows. For years now I've collected
bits of demolished kitchens, plumed majolica:
blaze-jagged, split-off designs. A burning house
as torch. My imagination lives in that
raging, put-out, abominated house,
where I should begin, stench and perfect dark
of soot, of saving, lost. The looking out
for what's not there. The houses that appear
to me in dreams, the rooms that come and go . . .
piles of porch, and when they shoveled it away,
the stray ash swirling. Even now I hear,
clear as good connections, after years,
the screened door scratch the stoop. But more of *air*
than *ground*. Bricks in spirals, closet, desk,
green rug of silky shoots, a magic land.
The house visits intermittently: bus ride
up a Tuscan hill, the garbage burning.
Scent that looks you up before plunging
back into that other continent
geographically incomprehensible,
geologically confused. Low, glass table
like the sleeping lady's coffin. Sinking couch
where we read Stevenson. Refrigerator

where the elephant I tried to believe in
tried to live. His blueness and pink splotches.
The pages that don't have to be turned again.
Flat of hand chopping spread into crack beneath
the pillows. Thin lawn beside the house before
other yards began. Dessert in the kitchen,
candles lighted. My father's painted studies
of black and white: a swimming sheet of bars
big as the wall. The beauty of an end
already finished. Incinerated book,
shelf of ash to set it back on. Being alive.
Deep winter hillside. Dim refrigerator bulb.
The glaze after the burning off of the spirit.
The want and the fullness. The smell in the air.

Notes

In "Caravaggio Paints *Narcissus*" "Both arsonist and scorched" was
taken from Narcissus' story in Allen Mandelbaum's translation of
The Metamorphoses of Ovid.

"Robert Capa's Last Photograph" is for Penelope Pelizzon.

"Matera" is for Valerie Haskell.